ADOPTED.

Thank you for
Making me feel
welcome!

Gloria Fuller

ADOPTED.

GLORIA FULLER

To my beautiful mother Lydia
and sweet little brother Gordon, who have made
me the person I am.

Table of Contents

Acknowledgements

Gordon, you have been my one and only best friend for a very long time. You've made me cry, but you've also been the one who wiped the tears from my eyes. This book is *our* book. Your past was hard, but I hope you can see that you are an overcomer.

Mom and Dad, you saved my life. I'm so glad that when I said "nothing," you came back and tried again. No matter how much I pushed you away, you came back. It's nice to know that someone in this world cares that much. If it weren't for you and God, this book would not have been written.

Skyler, Stormie, Tucker, Brooklyn, Thunder, and Lily, how can I thank you for sharing your parents, time, clothes, room, and so much more? When I was crying or angry, you supported me as much as you could. You bring so much fun into my life. I'm thankful for you and love you.

Barbara Sorrels, thank you for spending time with me when I first got to America and for helping Mom and Dad. You are a true miracle worker. You were the first person to think I should write a book. If you hadn't had my journals typed and bound, I would not have known that I could write a real book.

Mrs. Haynes, you were my first teacher and true friend at Christian Education Alliance. You cared about me, even in the tough times. One, two, three, and you were there. Thank you for helping with my book. You helped me believe I could be a writer. You encouraged me in so many ways.

Mrs. Ekhoff, you inspire me to be a better friend, student, writer—just a better person. I know that if you hadn't helped me edit this book, it would never have been published. Thank you for teaching me how to be a true author. I'm blessed to have you in my life. I love you very much.

I also want to thank the Haynes family and Jo Ann Craig for their edit of this book.

Hedwig, wow! Before you came into my life, my world was very small. I could never have dreamed about living with a bunch of white people and speaking English. Your ideas and hard work changed my life. Thank you for taking care of all the orphans. Many of us wouldn't be alive if it weren't for you. On behalf of all of us, thank you. I will love you always.

To my birth parents—Thank you for teaching me to work hard and pushing me to be a better person. Dad, Mom once told me that my face looks like yours. I'm proud that I have something of yours to carry with me. Mom, thank you for doing everything you could to keep the roof above our heads. I love you and miss you both so very much!

Foreword

I well remember the afternoon Julie Fuller shared her surprising news. She had recently been on mission trip to an orphanage in Uganda and had fallen in love with the children there. She and Greg were praying about adopting.

In the next year eleven-year-old Gloria and her three-year-old brother Gordon arrived in America. We all rejoiced with the Fuller family. We also grieved with them during the difficult adjustments that followed. As Julie's friend, I had the honor of praying for and with her at intervals. The Fullers are exceptional in transparency, faithfulness, and courage.

During this season Gloria began scribbling her new experiences and painful memories in a series of composition books. As she chronicled her story, she sensed the Lord's commission to publish a book.

In the year before Gloria became my writing student, family friend and counselor Barbara Sorrels suggested that Gloria write about her life. Later she tenderly received Gloria's journals containing parts of the narrative you are about to read and had them typed and bound into a booklet.

When Gloria became my student, she asked me to edit her book and make it "really good." As I much as I believed in her, I couldn't say yes—editing books can take years. Instead, I offered to write the foreword. Gloria was thrilled. She's delightfully easy to please.

In preparation to introduce Gloria to the reader, I downloaded her book into my computer, thinking I would scan the chapters and compose a heartfelt foreword. But I hadn't read far into her captivating story before Holy Spirit spoke, "You *will* edit this book." I answered simply, "Yes, Lord."

Since that decision, it has been my privilege to work beside Gloria, bringing out the deeper narrative and weaving the testimony. In the process I have found a hero in the author.

I place this really good book in your hands with confidence that the Lord is about to change your perspective—perhaps your life. There may be those who see the desperate need and decide to adopt. There may also be adopted kids and their parents, who find the courage to begin a "new ending." But this story transcends adoption. It contains profound wisdom for *all* who read on.

Susan Ekhoff
Gloria's editor, writing teacher, fan, and friend
11/17

Introduction

I'm growing up in a big family and sometimes I'm the kid who gets into trouble. But most of the time, I don't mean for that to happen. I have had times when I wished I were dead. And even tried to kill myself. Was that a great idea? No! But we all have our own problems.

I wasn't born here in America . . .

The Beginning

I lived in Uganda and, man, was that a hard life for me. When my parents died, that's when my life became awful. Let me tell you the whole story from the beginning.

I don't remember my father that much. My mom said I looked like him but had her eyes. All I remember about him is that he never wanted me to be in trouble or for my mom to get mad at me. Since I was the one and only kid, he gave me everything I wanted, which was actually fun. I fussed more than twenty times a day. Why? Just because.

But all that went away when my father died. He died when I was little. I didn't know that he had died until I was about seven. When I asked my mom where he went, she always lied to me and said that he was at work until one day she realized that she couldn't keep lying to me about my dad. So she told me that he had died. I was so sad and mad that I thought I would never talk to her ever again. I was wrong of course. As a matter of fact, that only lasted a couple of hours.

As I got older (I was about eight by this time), I knew that my mom kept that secret from me because she didn't want me to worry. I guess she was right not tell me because I did start to worry about things like—Who will make the money? Who will keep us safe in the house? Who will pay for me to go to school? Am I even going to go to school? —things like that. But my mom somehow took care of us.

My mom was pretty. She had big, brown eyes and lots of freckles. She had soft, high cheeks and long, dark hair. Sometimes she wore a scarf around her head or put flowers in her hair to match her dress. She taught me to push myself and never give up. She said, "Don't let people look down on you."

We lived in a cozy hut. The hut had a roof made of long grass. Inside was one room. My mom planted flowers beside the door: purple, yellow, pink, and white. We grew beans and plantains in the back. Grass and bushes grew all around, and there were some trees to climb. The weather was hot, hot, hot.

My mom was a good cook—especially chicken and rice. For a treat she made Ugandan hot chocolate, which is porridge made of flour, water, and sugar cooked together. I remember on Christmas night, we stayed up all night and some neighbors sang Christmas songs at our door. Sometimes we had tickle fights in bed.

But boy, could she get mad. Once I tried on her new necklace. I wanted to see if I could be pretty like her. But I broke the necklace. She spanked me hard. She spanked me a lot out of anger.

Adopted

My mom never learned anything. And she wasn't too excited about me learning anything either. I went to school for only one year. It cost a lot of money. The good thing was I made friends there. Sometimes the whole school had races in the field. I loved to run. But I didn't learn at school. When the teacher asked a question, *everyone* had to raise his hand. If you didn't know the answer, you hoped that she wouldn't call on you. I didn't know the answers, so I had to go pick out a stick for a beating. I found out that the big ones didn't hurt as much.

Then things changed. My mom kept getting sick. I think she got sick because she worked too hard. She had done jobs that men should do for long time. On sick days she had a headache or a fever. Sometimes she couldn't breathe. So she had to stay in bed a lot. When she felt better she could sew a little, but I had to do her harder jobs. That's when I stopped going to school. This was my list of things to do: get water, clean the house and make food, go dig, and get firewood.

First I had to get water. The well was three or four miles away. I carried the water home in my yellow "jerrycan," an African bucket. Sometimes I went with friends and sometimes I didn't.

Cleaning the house wasn't too bad; all I had to do was sweep the floor, wash the dishes with my hands, make the beds, and scrub the pots. I say it wasn't too bad because my house wasn't that big so I didn't have that many rooms to sweep and stuff like that. I made bean, rice, or vegetable soup. Sometimes I killed a chicken and roasted it over fire in the hut.

When I went to dig in someone else's field, my mom got paid. Digging started at seven in the morning, and I would come back home about three. I hoed the weeds around corn, potatoes or beans, or raked dirt up around the avocado trees to make sure they had enough dirt around the roots. But on digging days, I had some fun too. I would sometimes go to my best friend's house and have a sleepover. We stayed up all night and did whatever we wanted outside.

Getting firewood was probably the hardest chore because I had to go into the woods and cut wood with an axe and a handsaw. This was extra hard, especially being a girl.

My list stayed the same for a long time. When my mom saw how much I had to work, she changed the rules. She said that I didn't have to make food or dig if I didn't want to. I have to say that was a huge help. I knew that we needed the money so I made my very own garden. I sold things from my garden and bought some inside things. I bought myself a new dress and a pig for a pet. My mom was very proud of me.

When she started to get better, she saw how hard it was to be alone without a husband. She decided that since she was young, she was going to get married again. So she did. I hated the man she married, but I didn't tell her because I knew that she was doing the right thing.

A Baby Brother

My mom told me that she was going to have a baby. I was excited. But when the man my mom married heard that, he left the very next morning, and we never saw him again. A few months went by without his coming back, and Mom gave up on him.

The baby was getting ready to come. The problem was that in Uganda, people don't go to the hospital when a baby is born. I was starting to get worried because sometimes women die when they have babies. What if my mom died? What would I do? Thankfully, she didn't die.

Adopted

My brother was born at night on a Saturday. That Saturday morning, Mom went to dig. She worked hard all day. When we were eating dinner in bed, she started yelling. I asked her, "Are you alright?" She was in labor and needed help. She decided to go to a neighbor she trusted 3–4 miles away. I held the candle while we walked. When the wind blew it out, we walked in the dark. Mom was hurting so much that she crawled part of the way, and I walked behind to protect her. Just after we got into the neighbor's hut, the baby was born. If we had gotten there just one minute later, the baby would have been born in the street.

My mom called the baby *Gordon.* I was so happy to have a baby brother! I told everyone, even if it was people I didn't know—I didn't care.

After Gordon was born, my mom kept getting really sick. I raised him mostly by myself. Each morning, I fed Gordon and washed him. Then I wrapped him on my back with his baby blanket to go to the well. Sometimes the hills were too big so I rested. I cleaned the house and dug in the yard. I made the food and washed clothes.

Gordon was the cutest, chubby baby. We had a game where I lit a candle, and he followed it with his eyes. When I blew the candle out, he laughed. Gordon laughed a lot.

Then when I was about nine and Gordon was about nine months old, Mom got so sick that she went to the hospital. My grandma *Jujah* (jew-jə) paid for a motorcycle to take her. The hospital was in another town—three or four hours away.

Gordon and I lived alone in the hut for the next two months. We slept on our mattress together. I fed him soup or mashed bananas, beans, or potatoes, and gave him some milk. He called me *Goiya.* He only cried when he wanted Mom. It was hard to be a mom. I couldn't go out with other kids because I had a lot of responsibility. The kids didn't want to hang out with me anymore because I was a mom.

Adopted

We didn't have enough money to keep my mom in the hospital any longer so she was brought to my grandpa's house about ten miles away from our hut. I got Gordon ready and walked to Grandpa's to be with her. After a while my mom decided to sell our hut and move all our stuff to Grandpa's. It was hard for my mom and me, but she was worth it.

When my mom got better, she built a new hut next to Grandpa's house. She paid the uncles to cut small logs for the walls and long grass for the roof. She built the new hut herself by tying the logs together and covering the triangle roof with grass. She made some mud and filled in the holes between the logs. It was a nice new hut, and I liked it.

My mom's dad had a lot of kids because he had two wives. Sometimes it was fun to be with all the kids, but I got into fights with them a lot. That was okay, because I loved them. But they didn't love me that much. They didn't like Gordon at all.

Gordon and Me

My mom was struggling a lot more. She would breathe in long and slow, and breath out long and slow. It was so hard for her to breathe.

One Sunday night we were playing outside. (We didn't have a TV, so playing soccer and getting muddy was our fun.) Jujah came to me and said, "Your mom wants to talk to you." So I went inside.

Mom was lying on her pallet on the floor. Jujah left us to talk alone. Mom told me she was sorry for everything that she had done that wasn't nice. She kept talking in a hoarse voice, and I listened. She wanted me to promise that I would take care of Gordon no matter what happened. Finally she said, "Goodbye." —and then she died. I shook her, but she didn't wake up. I couldn't believe she was really dead and started crying—loudly. When the kids and Jujah heard me crying, they came in. They just stood and looked at me. Eventually, they sat down quietly.

It was dark, so finally the kids got ready and went to bed, but I didn't. Jujah checked on me throughout the night. But I stayed with Mom. I didn't sleep at all. I cried so hard that the next morning my face was all swollen.

In the years before my mom died, she had spanked me so much that I had sometimes wished she were dead. But now that she really was dead, I was sorry that I had thought that, and wished I could take it back. At first I thought it might be my fault that she had died, but now I know better—she died because of the hard work she did. I was kind of happy for her because she didn't have to work any more.

A lot of relatives and friends came. They stayed a day or two to comfort us. They brought food and said, "Poor girl."

The next day some of them built a wooden box and put my mom in it. They dug a hole. They read scriptures. I didn't want to, but everyone told me to throw a handful of dirt into the hole—I finally did. I wanted to fall into the hole too. After she was buried, a wooden cross was put at her grave.

After my mom died, Gordon and I lived in our hut by ourselves. I made sure that he had everything he needed. It was hard, but I knew if I didn't take care of him, he would die, and I would be alone.

Gordon cried every night wanting Mom. I told him that she had died, but he never understood what that meant. I cried when he cried. I cried because I wanted him to stop crying. I cried because I wished that Mom were still here. I wished it so much! Everything was a mess.

Mom died about a year after Gordon was born, when I really needed her.

Adopted

Gordon doesn't remember her at all. Sadly, Gordon had no idea what was going on. He has grown up without knowing his mother.

I guess Gordon finally got used to having me instead of Mom because he stopped crying. Gordon knew me as a mother and sister. We had fun with each other sometimes. I would make food, and we would take our pallet outside and eat on it. Then after we were done, we would jump on it. We played with my doll (like a corn husk doll, but made of dried plantain leaves) or my plantain soccer ball.

My mom's dad never liked us at all, even when my mom was still alive. He hated my mom so much, but I never knew why. She never told me, and that was good because I didn't think I wanted to know.

As time went on, I got tired of Gordon, and Gordon got tired of me. Gordon was now almost two years old. It might sound kind of silly, but he would bite me, and I would bite him back. He would slap me, and I would slap him back. The only good thing about it was that he stopped biting and hitting me because he knew I would get him back. Now, when I think about it, it was stupid of me to do that to him. We were good for a while.

Life at Grandpa's

When I told my mom's dad that I was scared of living in the house alone, he said that I could live with them until he found someone to live with me. He had a real house with mud walls. I thought that was really nice of him, but his kids could have been nicer. They were the type that threw rocks at people. And when I started to live with them, I became like them. I did what they did.

Most of the things we did were mean. When kids came by to go to school, we would make fun of their clothes, and they would start to cry because we hurt their feelings. We never cared! We thought it was funny.

Adopted

When we played capture the flag, we threw rocks at the trucks that came by. We liked to steal stuff from other people's fields— mangos, bananas, avocados, or pineapples.

It didn't take long until all of that was over. They turned on me and started to do some mean things that I will never forget. They kicked my chest until I started to bleed. They made me do their chores. I fetched the water, peeled potatoes, and cooked for them. I got the firewood, washed clothes, and cleaned the house. Every time I did their chores, I had to have Gordon on my back because they didn't want Gordon around. They said that if I didn't keep Gordon with me, they would kill him. I had to believe them. They had no mercy on anyone—not even each other. Grandpa went out drinking, and Jujah worked trying to earn some money. No one took care of the kids so they ruled themselves.

You would think that since I did the chores and made their food, I would be the first to eat. But actually, they picked the good stuff out and left me what they hated. They didn't give Gordon any food at all. So I gave Gordon some of mine. The leftovers didn't even fill Gordon up.

One day I told Grandpa about how the kids were being terrible to me, but he didn't make them stop. No, he actually told them to keep on doing what they were doing. When I did something wrong, he yelled and punched me or locked me out. When he was drunk, he would grab me and throw me out of his house and say, "Go where back where you belong." He hit me so bad sometimes, I couldn't walk. But I had to get up and keep going.

Every day I cried, "Why did Mom have to die?" The kids made fun of that. I hated everything they did to me. But most of all I hated when they hit Gordon. I tried to do anything to protect him. Sometimes I would say, "If you are going to hit Gordon, just hit me instead." They said, "Why do you care about him anyway? He's not even your *real* brother? You have a different dad than him." When I thought about it, I knew they were right. But he was still my brother, and I had promised Mom that I would take care of him no matter what. I guess she knew this would come.

Even though Gordon was kind of fat, I kept him on my back every single day no matter what. Even if the kids said they would babysit him, I always said *no.* I never knew what they might do to him. He was my one and only brother. I did whatever it took to keep him safe.

The best thing was when Gordon saw me crying. He would try to comfort me and say, "It's okay," and "I'll tell mom when she comes back." Sometimes, when I was really mad, I would yell, "Mom is gone! She's never coming back! You've got to understand that!" But Gordon couldn't understand. He always believed mom would come back. I knew the truth. We would never have a family that loved and cared for us. But somehow, Gordon always had hope.

My grandpa told me every day that I needed to find somewhere else to go so

I would stop eating his family's food. When he told me to find some place to be, I would think, "You're the one who's supposed to take care of us because you're our grandpa." Besides, we never really ate much of his food. He had a very big family and didn't have enough money to take care of them.

When people asked if I was okay, I told them I was. But it was a big, fat lie. I only did that because the kids told me not to tell anyone. They said that if I did, they would make my life even more terrible. I didn't know what more they could do, but I was too scared to say the truth.

One night, I couldn't take it anymore, and we left. When they woke up, Gordon and I were gone. They didn't know where we were for a long time.

We went first to my best friend's house. I thought her family would help us, but I was wrong. My friend asked her mom if they could keep us for just two or three days. Her mom said she would talk to her husband, but he said he didn't want anything to do with us. In the end, they just said, "Sorry," and walked away.

Everyone had been friendly when my mom was alive, but now it seemed like everyone was my enemy. That's the way it felt. I couldn't think of any place to go so I just started walking with Gordon on my back. I may have not known where we were going, but I knew for sure we were running away.

When people saw me crying and walking, they asked if I had anyone that should be taking care of us, and I told them about my grandpa. I told them I didn't want to go back to him. No matter what, I was *not* going back! So they asked me if I had any uncles. I told them that I did but one of them didn't have a house—he went everywhere and stayed wherever he wanted. The other uncle had a hut and kids, but he didn't like us. As a matter of fact, he had hated my mom so much that he told her that he never wanted to see her or us again.

Life with My Uncle

I talked to some people in the village, who thought I needed to go my uncle's house anyway. They made a plan. They found my uncle in town where he was drinking. They said, "If you don't take them, we'll tell the police, and you'll go to jail." So he said he would take us.

My uncle was a serious man. He didn't laugh much. He was a raggedy person, who didn't really care. I was afraid that if I went to my uncle's hut, I would be dead by morning. I thought of my mom, and how she and her brother didn't get along and fought with each other. I wondered, "How will my aunt treat me?" I didn't know what would happen, but I knew that the people were trying to help me, so I tried to be brave. Finally, I started walking toward his hut with Gordon strapped to my back.

After a long walk we to came the door. My aunt opened the door and we walked in. No one said anything to us, not even, "Why are you here?" or "Hey, would you like some food?" We really could have used some food. We'd left Grandpa's house during the night when everyone was asleep and hadn't had any food all day.

The hut had four little rooms and holes in the roof. There was a place for sleeping, a storage room, a sort of pantry that had salted meat on sticks in it, and a little room for everything else. They cooked outside unless it was raining. That was all. We were given a corner to sleep in.

The next morning my uncle went to work. His wife went to work too, but before she left, she gave me a list of things to do. Get the kids to school was the first thing. My uncle had only three kids. Two of them went to school and the little one was supposed to stay home with me.

I made some food for the kids to take, and we started out. I carried the year-and-a-half old girl. I had to leave Gordon at home because I couldn't carry them both. The school was in the city, 3 or 4 miles away.

When I got home, I made some food for us. I thought that I was allowed to have some and give some to Gordon. So I did what I thought was good. But when my aunt came home, she asked, "Did you give Gordon some food?"

"Yes."

Then she said the most hurtful thing. "You can eat, but Gordon can't."

When I asked why, she said, "He can't eat because he's not going to work. Since you're going to work every day, it's right for you to eat—unless you want to give *your* food to Gordon. Gordon's dad ran away and that's what he gets. If his dad hadn't run away, he could get food from his dad."

I didn't say anymore because I knew I would end up hearing something I didn't want to hear. I didn't want to hear her ideas about my mom and dad.

My aunt was tall and had short hair. She liked everything to be perfect. She told me what to do every day while I was living with her. She told me to go get water, get firewood, clean the house, go dig, wash the baby, make food, and go get the kids from school. "And don't forget you need to take the baby with you. And after you're done with everything, play with the baby." That sounded like an awful lot of things for a girl like me to do. I was glad that my mom had taught me how to work before she died. When my mom and I went to work, we had always taken Gordon with us. So I was used to that already.

While I worked, Gordon sat in that corner. No one played with him. You see, we both had ear infections that oozed. I was pretty good at hiding it, but he didn't know how. He just sat next to the door and sang or talked to himself.

Gordon and I slept on the pallet in the corner every night. Unfortunately, the roof leaked in that spot, so when it rained, we got pretty wet and cold.

I don't remember much about that time except the work, but there were a few fun things. Sometimes I played house with her kids. I had a plantain doll. I pretended her name was Lydia. I liked that name because it was my Mom's name. Every once in a while, we would invite our friends over and butcher a pig. The kids got to play with the left over parts while the parents cooked. Then we had a feast. Sometimes, if I did all my chores, and my aunt was in a good mood, she invited our friends over, and we played hide and seek in the dark. When she was in a bad mood she would yell at me, wrestle with me, or add more chores.

My aunt didn't want anything bad or hard to happen to *her* kids. The other two children were about 9 and 10. You would think they would be old enough to help with chores—but no, they didn't. All they did when they came home was get a snack and go out to play at their friends' house. Sometimes their mom gave them chores, but they usually didn't do them. When they didn't get their chores done, I would get in trouble. Since I was oldest, I was responsible for what they did. But how can you be responsible for kids who won't listen to you?

My aunt said things like, "Why didn't you tell them to do their chores?"

"You told me not to tell them what to do."

"Well, why didn't *you* do the chores *for* them?"

I would say, "I was too busy with *my* chores."

She would say, "I didn't give you that much to do when I left. So what were you doing this whole day?"

When she said that, I couldn't say anything more, so I said that I wasn't doing anything. Then she would add more chores for me to do. I think my aunt thought I was a selfish, bratty snitch. She thought I was a lazy, no-good. When she was in a good mood, she didn't really talk to me. I liked her better when she didn't talk. Later, when I heard the story of Cinderella, I knew how she felt.

My uncle never knew what was going on with me because he was not home much. He was a hunter. He came home late and left early, or he and his friends spent the night in the woods. They sold the meat they killed and brought some home—deer, wild goats, pigs, and monkeys. When I realized that he wouldn't be at home most of the time, I was glad.

The truth was he cared for us a little bit, and here's how I found out: One time I had done something really bad, and my aunt wanted to spank me, and they fought over it. "Even Gloria needs a little time without being spanked," he said.

Then I thought, "Maybe he does care but doesn't know how to show it."

Another time I didn't finish my chores because I had so many, and everyone was eating except Gordon and me. My uncle asked, "Why aren't they eating?"

And his wife said, "Because Gloria didn't do all her chores.

So he said, "Is that right?"

She said, "Yes."

Then he asked, "Who made this food?"

She said, "Gloria did."

"Well?" he said. He started to talk about how much I had been working. Then he made his way inside, got Gordon and me a plate full of food, and gave it to us. My aunt didn't like that. She was mad. The next morning she gave me an even bigger list of chores. Still, what my uncle did that night was the nicest thing that anyone had done for me for a long time.

My uncle told his wife that she could do anything to me but hurt me. And he said the same for Gordon. But my aunt hurt Gordon a lot when my uncle wasn't around. She did that because he couldn't speak. He was just a baby. I wanted to tell my uncle, but I didn't—for one thing I wasn't allowed to, and for another, I never really saw him.

A Strong Faith

In all the bad times, I was a still a Christian. My Mom had raised me to be a Christian when she was alive. I knew that people like me that sin a lot can be forgiven. I believed in God, but I couldn't understand why He didn't just make all the horrible things stop happening. Now I know that bad things happen to good people too. It was hard for me to live a Christian life when I wasn't in a Christian home any more.

The people I lived around *said* they were Christians, but they didn't act like it. The way they dressed and spoke to each other seemed wrong. Maybe they were confused Christians, but I don't think they believed what was true. They mixed up ideas about the true God with stuff they thought up. They believed that a god made everything and everybody, but he was so old that he had no teeth. I didn't believe that God was old and weak, but they said as long as I lived with them, I had to believe what they believed. So I did—well, I acted like it.

Their god had given them some special water to drink when they got sick. It was kept it in a milk jug and the jug was refilled at church each week. It was supposed to make you feel better. When I got sick that's what I had to drink. It never worked on me. So when I got sick, I didn't tell anyone because I didn't like drinking that stuff. It tasted bad.

The kids could tell when I was sick anyway because my eyes would get kind of yellow looking. That's the way people look when they have malaria. I had to be in the sun because I felt cold and queasy all the time. But when I was sick, I had a little fun too. My uncle would give me a couple of cents to buy some stuff, and I got the day off—all because of my uncle.

My uncle also said everyone should have Sunday off. But my aunt managed to change his mind on that. Thankfully, Sunday's work wasn't that hard. I just washed the kids' uniforms, cleaned their shoes, and cut their nails.

When we went to their church, we didn't take Gordon with us. He stayed home alone. I had to carry my aunt's baby to church and couldn't carry Gordon too. I didn't want him to stay home when we went somewhere fun. So when it was time to go to church, I acted like I was sick so they would have to leave me at home with him. When they saw that I was sick almost every Sunday, they started taking Gordon and leaving me at home. I thought, "Well, that's new." But some of my friends told me that when they took Gordon to church, they hurt him really bad. That made me mad because he was just little. So on Sundays, I didn't get sick anymore so I could go to church instead of Gordon.

One time my aunt and I were going to get some food from the garden and I asked her a question. "Since you believe in that old man who is supposed to be god, and I don't, then who do you think made *me*?"

She was quiet for a minute, and then she said, "Do you see that big tree over there?"

I said, "Yeah."

Then she said, "That's who made you."

I thought that was the funniest thing, so I started to laugh. But when I looked at her face, she looked serious. So I said, "Okay." In my mind I didn't believe it. It sounded too silly. My mom had told me that God is the only one who can make humans.

Protecting Gordon

My aunt hated me, and she told everyone—but she hated Gordon more. This is what happened: Since my uncle didn't come home from work that much, she put Gordon in the bush (a place near the house that was kind of like the jungle, all filled with trees and bushes) and left him there all day and sometimes all night—even if it was raining. I wasn't supposed to go check on him because I was supposed to be working, but I did anyway. I brought him food or would steal a blanket and bring it to him. When the kids were at school or the baby was taking a nap, I would stay in the bush and play.

Adopted

One night Gordon was outside alone in the rain. He wasn't crying or anything. He was just sitting there doing nothing. I was in the house crying because Gordon was out there alone.

Sometimes wild dogs would come out at night, looking for something to eat. Suddenly, we heard dogs howling outside. I cried harder and harder when I heard them. My aunt and her kids laughed at me. They thought the dogs wouldn't hurt him, and it was silly to cry, but I knew those dogs could eat just about anything—even people. I was so scared.

I started yelling at my aunt, saying how mean she had been, and what I was going to do if she ever left her baby with me and expected me to take care of her again.

Finally, I shoved her out of my way, opened the door, and ran out to save Gordon. My aunt grabbed me and started hitting me with her hands. I was crying, and Gordon got up and started crying. When she finally let go, she started toward Gordon to hit him, too, but I grabbed him before she could reach him, and together we ran further into the bush. My aunt went back toward the house. As she shut the door, she shouted back that I was not allowed in the house. After a while Gordon and I crept out and sat on the ground next to the door, crying.

Then I heard my uncle coming home. My aunt must have heard him, too because she opened the door for Gordon and me to come inside. She didn't want to get into trouble. But my uncle saw us, and asked, "Why are you crying?"

Before I could answer, my aunt jumped in and started telling him all these things that didn't really happen. She lied until my uncle believed what she was saying. He got mad and grabbed my hands. He was about to start hitting me, but something stopped him. He said, "Gloria, I am not going to hurt you."

My aunt said, "Why?"

My uncle never told her why. I was amazed. Even though I had marks on me from where my aunt had just hit me, he said, "*I'm* not going to hit you."

I was so glad, and I could tell that Gordon was glad, too because when we got in our bed, he kept saying that he was glad that I didn't get spanked.

Our bed was wet because of the rain. We couldn't sleep too well, but my side wasn't as wet so I let Gordon sleep close beside me.

The next day I started on my chores as usual. The kids went to school, and my aunt went to work. My aunt took the baby with her so I was happy. My uncle was the last to leave the hut. Before he left, he warned me, "If I were you, I would leave this house for good before every one gets home."

I thought about it, and then said to Gordon, "He's right." So I strapped Gordon on my back with his blanket, and we left for good.

As we walked along, I decided to go to this old lady who was my mom's friend, and ask her what to do. She lived about twenty minutes away. She had a real house with a tin roof. When we got there, she seemed to know what we had been through. She said, "You are too small because you haven't been eating enough. You can stay with me."

Everything began to change for Gordon and me from that moment.

Rescued

This lady got us food and drinks. The clothes we were wearing were kind of ripped all over so the next day she made us new ones. She gave us a room with a bed—a real bed. And she said, "You can call me Grandma, or Mom, or anything that sounds good to you."

I was so happy, but I still had problems. Sometimes I didn't get along with her kids. But I still had to help them cook, dig, and all the other chores. I worked as much as they did. Still, it wasn't too bad compared to what I had been doing. Gordon and I were alone for some of the day, but things were better.

Adopted

Another problem was that Grandma drank every night. Sometimes she was nice when she was drunk. She asked, "Do you need anything?" Whatever I said I wanted, she gave me.

When she was really drunk she acted strange and talked too much. She would make her youngest son George (who was a little older than me) and me get out of bed—even when we were sleeping. She gave us some beer or whatever she was drinking, and she would tell us we had to drink it too. And we would. She would also keep us awake for a long time telling us stories that we already knew. Then she put us in the guest bed. We hated it. I was a girl, and he was, well, he was a he. We both hated that.

Finally, we asked, "Can we go back to bed?" She would let us, but before we could even close our eyes, she would get us up and start talking again. We usually took a nap the next day, but I hated that she made us drink.

Sometimes she would get drunk during the day too. And that was not good because then she wanted me to do things that I didn't know how to do. She was the village doctor so she told me to go find stuff for medicines, but I didn't know what to look for.

After a while Grandma trained me in ways to help people get well. She never spanked me the whole time I lived with her.

One night Grandma came into the kitchen and grabbed my hand. When someone grabbed my hand, it usually meant I was in big trouble. But this time was different. She took me into her room and closed the door. She said, "I know you've been through so much, but I was wondering if you want to learn?"

I said, "I do, but who would take care of Gordon? So, no thank you."

Then she said this: "Don't worry about Gordon any more, I will take care of him, and we will have fun together!" I started to smile and smile. I was so happy that I said, "YES!"

She said, "Tomorrow, I will buy you notebooks, a lunch box, and a uniform, and you can go to school next week." I started to cry. And for the first time, it was tears of joy.

The next morning I went to her and said, "Grandma? Did you really mean what you said last night?"

She said, "Yes! I was drunk, but I still knew what I was talking about." I thanked her so much, and she smiled at me.

In the next days I watched her play with Gordon, wash him, and feed him, and I thought, "Wow, someone actually cares about us."

When I started school, it was great. Right away, I re-met this boy who had been a friend before my mother died. We liked to walk to school together.

It was fun at the school. My teacher described things. Most teachers expected you to know stuff already, but he explained the math problems and English words. I liked him.

My school was small and dusty with a thatched roof. There were three classrooms with about twenty kids in each one, and two teachers. The class that didn't have a teacher just played outside until it was their turn to learn. The kids sat on the floor. We had a chalkboard at the front of the room. The teacher spanked us, but not so hard and not so much.

There was one thing I didn't like about school. Some of the kids bragged about how great their life was and how much money they had. They knew that I was the only one there without parents and made fun of me. It made me miss my parents more and know that I wasn't smart. It just hurt.

About twelve weeks went by. Then I had to stop going to school because the teachers quit. There were too many kids for just two teachers, and they wanted to be done with teaching. They said they weren't getting paid enough. I missed school, but I was also glad to be home.

Bless the Children

One night about two months later, Grandma was listening to the radio and she heard this guy say that if anyone had kids that didn't have parents, they could bring them to this orphanage where kids could get "sponsored." She told me that I was going to the orphanage the very next Sunday. It was full of kids who didn't have parents just like me. And I was going to go to school there—even Gordon!

On Sunday morning, my grandma's grown-up daughter came from where she lived to take us. We rode with this guy on his motorcycle. He rode in the front, next came Gordon, then me, then Grandma's daughter. It was a long ride.

As we came near the ministry, we could see a church on the hill surrounded by jackfruit, avocado, and mango trees. At the entrance there was a sign that said, "Welcome to Bless the Children Ministry."

The orphanage was as big as two giant football fields. There were three long classrooms with walls and tin roofs, and two small fields—one for girls to play on and a separate one for boys (who can be rough) to play soccer.

When we got there, it was Sunday so the people were still in church. When they were finished, Hedwig and Pastor Francis came to us and talked for a while. Hedwig and Pastor Francis were the ones who started the ministry so they were the bosses.

Hedwig seemed nice. She was short and stout with a medium Afro. But I could tell she was strict.

Pastor Francis was big, very dark-skinned, and bald. His flat nose had sweat beads on it. He had a booming voice and looked mad. I was afraid of him because he looked a lot like some men who used to get drunk, break into our house, and push my mom around. It didn't seem like Pastor Francis really cared about us.

After talking for a while, Hedwig said, "This is the plan: You will stay here forever." When she said that, I felt kind of sad. I didn't have any friends here, and I couldn't speak their language (dialect).

When everything was finally settled, Grandma's daughter left Gordon and me at the orphanage. Gordon and I were alone for a while until Hedwig brought us to my new house mom, who was called "Aunt Lydia." She carefully cleaned the "jingers" out of our feet. (You get bugs in your feet from walking barefooted in the bush.) Then she fed us. She was smart, pretty, and always smiling. It was hard for her to stay angry with anyone. She encouraged me to try new things and learn about God. She said, "This world is not all about lollypops. It's a hard a world."

Adopted

I got to sleep with Gordon one last time before moving to the girl's dorm. After that I was lonely because I didn't make new friends right way. It was hard for me to learn another language, and the food wasn't the best—but it was lots better than not eating. Aunt Lydia helped me to see I could do these hard things.

I started school right away. At first I was put in the 4th grade, but because of not going to school that much and learning different things, I was sent back. The 3rd grade teacher said that I didn't know anything, and sent me to 2nd grade. The kids laughed at me because I wasn't smart. I was mad. Thankfully, I stayed in second grade. In this school you stayed in the same class for two years before moving up. I was the oldest one in the second grade and this embarrassed me so much. I had homework, and it was hard, but I tried to learn.

Our teachers always wanted us to raise our hand when they asked a question—even if we didn't know the answer. When we didn't know the answer, we got spanked all over. They just swung a stick and whacked. It didn't matter if you were biggest or the smallest one in the whole school. (This is the way school has been done in most places in Uganda for a very long time, but I've heard that since we were there BTCM is changing this.)

We had to speak English anytime we weren't in class. If you were caught not speaking it, you got a card, and after dinner you were spanked so much. I had no idea how to speak English so I didn't talk a lot. When I did talk, I just said *yes* or *no.* Speaking English was really hard on the kids, especially the little ones. They didn't learn English in school, but still had to speak it. Some of the house moms said you had to speak English—even if you didn't know it. But Aunt Lydia didn't make us. She was awesome.

We also did chores at the orphanage—lots of chores. Sometimes, if we didn't do the chores, we couldn't eat. Chores in Uganda—they're really hard. But I got used to them like I always had.

When some people from America came to see us, we got excited. But we ended up not seeing them because we were locked in the house. The house moms didn't want us to be with them because they thought they didn't come to see us. Americans just wanted to see the school and orphanage. We were dirty and would bug them. But when Hedwig heard about it, she told the house moms not to do that again because the guests were there to see us kids.

It was really fun being with people that told me that they loved me even if I couldn't speak English with them. I could tell that they loved me by little things. They hugged me and let me touch their hair. They gave me candy and balloons—things that some people take for granted—that's what they did for us.

There was still one thing that didn't seem right. Most everyone had a sponsor, and I didn't. Every time kids got stuff from their sponsor, I wondered, "Am I going to have a sponsor that sends notes, pictures, candy, and all that?" Gordon eventually did, and I was happy for him. When his sponsor sent him candy, he shared it with me. For a long time I wished to have a sponsor of my own. Finally, I got one. She never got to come see me, but she sent stuff and notes that said, "You are loved." The visitors and my sponsor were the first people I ever heard say, "I love you."

Meeting My Parents

After many months Hedwig told me something surprising. She said, "A family wants you and Gordon to become part of their family." I didn't believe her for a long time. I thought, "Who in the world wants orphanage kids that don't even have three outfits, or three pairs of underwear?" I didn't know that was *why* they wanted us to a part of their family. They wanted to take care of us. I just couldn't believe it.

One day Hedwig came to me and said, "Do you want to go live in America?" I didn't know what to say because (1) I had heard so many stories about white people eating black people, but at the same time (2) I imagined living in America with cool, rich people would be great. So without thinking about it I said, "Yes! But if I go, I want Gordon to come with me." I didn't want to go without Gordon. We'd been through so much together. She said, "Great, because they're coming to get you and Gordon very soon!"

This was important news for Gordon and me. Kids in BTCM sometimes went to live in America, but I never thought I'd go. It sounded good—well, if they didn't eat us. That whole week kids around me said goodbye. They said, "They will eat you first and then Gordon." I got scared, but I knew that God was going to be with us no matter what.

Not long after this, I was in class doing the hardest subject ever—reading—when a house mom came in and told the teachers that I had to be done with school. Greg and Julie were coming. They were the people, who wanted Gordon and me to come with them to America. All the kids in my class said, "You're lucky. You don't have to do reading."

The house mom told me that I needed to shower and get dressed. We showered in the bush, but we had showers that were inside for visitors. That day I got to shower inside. It was my first time to use that type of shower. I thought that it was the coolest thing. But I had to shower fast because Greg and Julie were on their way!

Gordon and I quickly got ready and went to where they were waiting. Julie didn't look anything like my mom. She was pale, and she had long, light-red hair. Her eyes were pretty and blue. She looked healthy. Greg was a bigger person than I expected. He was bald. I didn't expect that because a lot of Americans had long hair. I thought that being bald was a Ugandan thing. Dad was ready to party! He seemed excited, but nervous. Mom looked nervous too, but happy. When they talked, they had a strong accent and talked fast.

We spent the whole day with them so we could get to know each other.

Adopted

Gordon liked them right away because he got candy and toys. I thought that they were the strangest people I'd ever seen. They were so white and their language sounded strange. I didn't say much for a while. I used gestures mostly. Hedwig was our translator. After a while I got used to them.

Then things got really good. They gave us clothes, and I got pants too. It was my first pair of pants. I also got a long, purple dress.

Not only did we eat with them, but we all slept in the same room. Hedwig had said, "You should start to call them *Mom* and *Dad* because that's the closest relationship you could ever have, and it will make them happy." I'm pretty sure it did.

I couldn't speak to them in English. If I wanted something, I had to show them to make them understand. But soon enough, I started to learn some new words from my new parents: yes, no, bath, thank you, and I love you, too.

Gordon and I skipped school to go places with them—fun places like restaurants and shops. We even drove to Hedwig's house. They had so much money! I got to have anything I wanted. It felt like heaven.

When a person from BTCM lined everyone up to cut our hair, my new mom said something to Hedwig that might have sounded like, "What are they doing?" Hedwig told her what was happening, and she asked if they could leave my hair long. Hedwig told her that if I wanted, I could. My new mom came to me and said, "How would you like to leave your hair long?"

Of course, I said, "I would love that."

I thought, "Wow! Am I really going to keep my hair long just like my new mom's?"

We lived together at BTCM for about a week, and then went to Kampala, the capital of Uganda, for many weeks. At the first hotel we got eaten up with mosquitoes, and it was terrible. But the next morning we went to a different hotel that was a lot better—clean and huge. Gordon and I shared a big room with a queen-sized bed. Later, we stayed in another hotel with other families who were adopting kids.

My parents gave us new clothes almost every day. We got dressed and then ate breakfast. And breakfast was good. We ate and watched TV at the same time. After breakfast we went places, and the places were great. Sometimes it all felt like a dream that was going to end. But it didn't. It really was me having *fun.*

During our time in Kampala, my parents worked on our government papers, and we talked to a judge. The judge asked Gordon and me some questions. "Are your parents really dead? Do you want to go with these people? Do you really want to live in America?"

I could tell Gordon wanted to go because he seemed to like the candy and the parents. I wasn't sure I wanted to start a new life—new friends, new home, new siblings, new everything.

But I knew that this was my first and last chance to make a change with people who really cared about me. I could go to a real school. I could learn the things I needed to know. I knew I had two choices: "Yes, I would love that," or "No, I want to stay, and live and die like my parents." That's when I answered, *"Yes."*

The judge also wanted to see the person who sent us to BTCM, so Grandma met with us. The judge asked us a lot more questions like: "Is this the person who took care of you? Was she nice?"

When we were done, Gordon and I got to sit with Grandma and say goodbye to her. This boy from BTCM, one of my best friends, had given me a little money because I helped take of him when he was sick. I had it with me. So when we were saying goodbye to Grandma and were about to leave, I gave her the money. She asked, "Why?" All I said was, "This is for you." I wanted to say thank you for everything. I think she loved it.

Adopted

The next day Mom gave me a special doll. It had the same color skin as me and long hair. Dad gave Gordon a tiger. We loved them and took them everywhere we went. In the meantime I was thinking, "What will America be like?

Welcome Home

After a few weeks Dad flew back to America so he could go back to work while Mom stayed to get us ready to leave Africa. All the time I kept wondering if the kids in America would like me. The more I thought about it, the more I worried.

The next thing I knew, Mom said, "I have some news to tell you. Today we leave for America." The whole time I was packing, I was thinking, "This is cool, and crazy, and scary at the same time."

Mom told me that we were going to fly in the air. I had never been on such thing as a plane. When we took off, I thought I was going to pass out. My stomach started to feel weird. But I got used to it very soon.

Gordon and I watched movies on the plane. It helps to know the language when you watch movies. I didn't, so I just watched for fun. I saw *Peter Pan, Tangled,* and *Cinderella.* I didn't know about magic or fairy-tales, so I was kind of confused.

We flew all night. The next morning we ate breakfast on the same plane. When we finally landed, and it was time to change planes, people were everywhere. I was afraid I was going to get lost, so I stayed close to Mom. We had to wait for a long time for the second plane. Things were beginning to be different because I didn't see many black people anymore. I thought, "What if they turn on me and eat me?" After a while I saw that I was safe.

The next time we landed, we walked forever. Mom walked so fast it was hard to keep up with her. Thankfully Gordon was in a baby cart, so he was fine.

The last plane was a lot smaller, and we got to sit wherever we wanted. I wanted to sit next to a window, so I sat across from Gordon and Mom. While we were flying, I got this feeling that said, "Hey, why don't you open the window shade and look out?" I was happy to see the clouds. I kept on looking and looking at them until my stomach started to feel sick, and my head started to hurt. Then I closed the shade.

When I opened the shade the next time, I saw big buildings that were beautiful. Mom told me that we were about to land. It was finally time to see my new family. Mom explained that people were going to cry when they saw me, but it would be because they were happy. As she was saying this, she was crying too.

When we got off the plane, there was my new family. I had six new siblings: Skyler was oldest (16). Next there was Stormie (15), Tucker (14), and Brooklyn (9). Lily and Thunder (7) were twins. Their grandma was in town to meet us. There were lots of new friends, too. They all started hugging us. In Uganda we don't hug. It felt weird, but I figured that's the way they show someone they love them. They gave us balloons and other surprises. It was a great welcome home party.

When it was time to go to our house, we went in a car, and the things I saw were amazing. I saw roads that were on top of each other. What if we fell? Thankfully, we didn't.

When we got out of the cars at home, Dad said, "Welcome to your new family!" He had a great, big smile on his face. We all went into the house together.

It was a big house. The girls showed me my bedroom and my bed. Everything looked so new. My bed had a stuffed tiger and a card that said *Gloria* on it. I got my own pillow and sheets. I'd never had sheets or a pillow before (except at the hotels, of course).

Then I started to cry. It was partly because I wasn't going to see my

Ugandan friends for a long time, and partly because I was happy to finally be at my new home. When it was time for dinner, I didn't want to eat. I said to myself, "I'll wait until I go back to Uganda. I don't know what's in this food."

Our new siblings were nice to us. They took us out to play on their trampoline. My older sister Skyler helped me take a shower. After that I remember Brooklyn telling Thunder that he should let me sit in the comfy chair to watch a movie. When he did, I sat on it. The next thing I knew, Skylar was waking me up and putting me in my bed. I was so tired that when Mom and Dad came in to say good night, I was asleep.

Over the next days I found out a lot of things that were different from Uganda. For one thing, I didn't see people walk places. When they did, it was because they just wanted to get some exercise. I saw that you didn't have to go get the water because water was already in your house. That made me so happy because I hated getting water. We didn't even go get firewood. You don't really need firewood if you have a stove. You just turned it on and off. But my favorite thing was the washing machine. You put clothes in, waited for a while, and the clothes were clean. Everything was new. My whole new life had begun.

Healing

Everything was new, but that didn't mean that everything was perfect. Being adopted is not something that can be easy. It takes bravery.

Not long after I came to my new family, I started to have problems again. I was angry a lot. I hated school. I missed my old life.

I couldn't talk about my feelings for a long time. Finally, Mom and Dad took me to a counselor. I hated counseling too and decided not to talk. Mom and Dad said, "The more times you won't say anything, the more times you'll have to go to counseling. You've had so much happen to you. You need to talk about it all with someone." I thought I knew better than they did and still wouldn't say anything. The truth was I was afraid to talk. When I talked about stuff in Uganda, people said, "You're silly. You don't know what you're talking about." I also thought that if I talked, the counselor would tell Mom and Dad all the bad things I had done.

Things just kept getting worse. I didn't want to play with other kids because I thought, "They don't want to hang out with me, and I don't blame them because I'm a jerk." I felt fat and ugly so I stopped eating so I could be skinny like my siblings. Then I started taking lots of naps, all in one day. I shared a room with Lily and Brooklyn. Lily had the top bunk, and I was on the bottom. I found some ways to make a fort out of my bed so no one could see me. Sometimes I put up signs that said, "Go away!" or "Nobody is home." If Lily came into the room, I could hear the paper being crumpled up and thrown into the trashcan. I stayed in my room because I hated myself and everyone else.

All this caused me to hate God as well. Everyday I would write in my journal about how much I hated me, everyone, and God. When I prayed, I wasn't afraid to let God know how I felt. Sometimes my prayers sounded like this: Dear God, I hate myself a lot! I want you to send someone who is brave enough to kill me. Or you can do it Yourself—whichever is easier. Make it snappy. P.S. I hate You too." Sometimes my prayers were nice and short. "Dear God, why couldn't you have killed me instead of my parents?"

When God didn't kill me, the day came when I decided to take matters into my own hands. That day I cried so much that my tears stopped coming. Even though I didn't want to leave Gordon alone without his real family, I tried to kill myself.

I had some more counseling after that, but soon I was worse than ever. I started having nightmares about the horrible things that happened to me back in Uganda. I started hearing and seeing things, and feeling like someone was always watching me. Things started to feel scary. I was afraid to tell anyone without sounding crazy. This whole thing went on and on. Finally, I couldn't take it any more. I told my brother Tucker that I wanted to kill myself. Once again the news went to Mom and Dad. They told me that they were proud of me for telling someone.

My parents took me to Parkside, a hospital for people who are hurting and can't get better. I lived there for two and a half months. I think it saved my life. After being there for a while, I got some meds that helped me with depression and Post-traumatic Stress Disorder (PTSD). When they explained what all that was, I wasn't surprised. Then I began to talk about my past more. I saw that I got hurt by others and hurt others as well.

At first I was ashamed that I had to take the medicine and had PTSD. But my mom explained that the reason I was so sad and angry in the first place was because I was hurt. She said, "It's OK to take medicine for *help*." I'm learning that it is OK to need help.

When I was adopted, I had to ask myself some questions: Am I really ready to let other people take care of me? Do I deserve for someone to take care of me? What if I mess up?" I liked to act hardheaded and tough. But I had to learn that it's not a sign of weakness to need help. Now I am learning to let God into my hurt.

I still struggle with school, fitting-in, concentration, jealousy, flashbacks, and I could go on and on. What I struggle with most is worrying. I sometimes worry about whether I'm good enough for people to like me. I worry about becoming a terrible mom. Yes, I know you're probably thinking, "You're not even married yet! How can you worry about that?" But that's the way my brain works. I worry about the day Gordon wants me to tell him everything there is to know. I don't want to answer questions like, "What happened to Mom and Dad?"

I guess I have a habit of holding on to the past. Sometimes I even find myself scared of the past. But what I need to remember is this quote I heard from Maria Robinson. It goes like this: "Nobody can go back and start a new beginning, but anyone can start today and make a new ending." I can't go back and start my life over, but I have decided to go on toward my new ending. I'm letting people help me and finding out that I can help them too.

I am also learning to trust God. Looking back I can see that He was with me the whole way. When I didn't have a father—He was my Father. When I didn't have friends—He was my Friend. When I thought I was loosing everything—He stayed by me. Now I know He will be with me forever.

Letters to My Parents

Mom,

Out of everyone in the family, I owe you the most apologies. I've given you the worst attitudes and even ignored you for weeks and weeks—but you still love me every day. You work hard for my siblings and me, but somehow keep a great attitude. I've never seen such a selfless, godly woman like Julie Fuller. What most people don't see is how brave, funny, and intelligent you are. You are a giver. You hug me when I'm tired of life.

I know it hasn't been easy, but you keep trying to help me with school. I remember when I was learning to read. I cried every time I had to read something out loud to you. I thought that I would never be able to read. But, Mom, you stayed by my side. You kept helping me. You never gave up on me, and you still haven't. Thank you for giving your time. I love you.

Adopted

Dad,
I couldn't have a better dad than I have right now. You paid thousands of dollars to come across the ocean and get Gordon and me. You paid lots of money for all my doctors' bills. You are a hard-working man. Thank you for working three jobs to keep us all fed.

Without you I wouldn't be spending my life with a family that loves and cares for me. If I had to choose to have you as my hero or my dad, I think I would choose you to be my dad. You are so good at putting up with all my drama. I am greatly thankful for that. I love you to the moon and back.

Some of my favorite phrases that you say to me are, "You need to understand that I'm pulling for you," and, " I would do all of that mess again just for you." I am so glad that I'm your daughter. Thank you for pushing me to do my best. I love you.

Thoughts

For People Who've Been Hurt

I had a lot of hard things happen to me in Uganda. I sometimes cry because I'm mad at God for letting my mom die and for letting my grandpa and other people, who took care of Gordon and me, be so mean. Some of the people that should have taken care of us—they rejected us instead. I don't really blame them now because they didn't know what to do, and they didn't have much to help us with.

When I go back to Uganda, I am planning on bringing a lot of things for my family, like clothes and candy, because they don't even know what that is, and they might eat the wrappers too! But that's not the point. The point is for me to go there and just bless them even though they didn't really bless me. That's what my heart feels like God wants me to do. You can bless people even when they've hurt you.

Maybe you are hurting right now. I want you to know that no matter how many bad things are happening, there's always a bright side. Hurt people can be thankful for *something*. During my hard times I didn't feel like there was a bright side, but the truth was that we could have died, but didn't. That means that some good things were happening, too. Bad times come, but there is always a way out.

For Adopted Kids

The day my mom died, I had no hope. I wasn't planning on being alive for long. I thought Gordon and I would die of starvation, and we almost did. I was always afraid that Gordon would die before I did because he got sick so much, and I didn't have any medicine to give him. Sometimes I tried to kill myself so that I wouldn't have to watch Gordon die first or have to take care of him. I ended up with scars everywhere—on my legs and arms, but mostly on my heart. But God helped me make it though.

When Hedwig told me that I was going to have a new family that cared about me, I thought, "What is this family thinking by choosing *me?* I mean, are they crazy?" It turned out that they weren't crazy—just crazy fun. I wasn't the smartest kid. I wasn't the nicest kid. But parents who adopt kids don't love them for what they can do. They love them because they are fearfully and wonderfully made.

Adopted kids all have different stories, but we understand each other. We understand what it's like to say goodbye to our parents and start all over with a new family.

If you're adopted, I hope you'll remember that God sent Jesus to the earth to save the broken ones. And we're the broken ones—all of us. We all need Jesus.

The Lord's got your hand, and He won't let you fall. He has a great big family, and you can be a part of it. I hope you will let Him help you. He always loves you.

For People Who Wonder If They Should Write Their Story

When I decided to write this book, I wasn't sure if I could do it. Writing is hard and takes a long time. But people kept saying, "Gloria, your story is going to be great; you should write it." Even though this is only half of my story—letting the whole world know *everything* about me didn't make me feel good inside—still, I decided to write what I could.

Before the book was finished, satan tried to tell me that I wasn't good enough to write a real book, and no one would read it. He said, "Everyone will make fun of you because your book is so short." I believed him at first, but the people that cared about me kept saying, "Gloria, your story matters, and people will like it." My sister Skyler told me, "satan is going to try to make you feel bad about yourself, then make the lie sound like God." I knew this was true because he had already tried to fool me with other foolish thoughts. That's when I realized that it doesn't really matter how long a book is. What matters is what's inside the book, and how it can change people's lives.

I had many ideas about what to name my story. Then I realized it wasn't my choice to write it in the first place— it was all God's idea. So I asked Him, "What should I name this book that you asked me to write?" He gave me an answer: *Adopted.* Then I thought, "Maybe that's just me thinking that." I prayed again, and He gave me the same answer. So I took it. I've been *adopted* into the Fuller family, and I've been *adopted* into the Lord's family.

My story matters and so does yours. There may be people who need to read your story before their story can get better. I think you should write it.

For people who want to know more about Jesus

Without Jesus, we are far from God, and there's no way to change that. But God sent Jesus to die for our sins on a cross and rise up again. The good news is that we can lay down our burdens and sins and accept Him as our Savior. After that He lives *in* us. The old of us is gone and the new of us has come.

If you want, you can pray about all this by saying: God, I know I'm a sinner and there's nothing I can ever do to change that. Thank you for sending Jesus to die in my place so I can be Your child. I give You my broken life and take Your life instead. Come live in me and make my life new. Amen

I'm happy that Jesus lives in me. He is teaching me how to treat other people like He treats me. I never have to be scared that He doesn't love me. I ask Him questions. He's my best friend.

One day when I die, I'm going home to Heaven to the place Jesus has made for me. I'm excited because my mom and dad are waiting for me there.

"For God so loved the world that he gave his one and only Son, that whoever believes in him shall not perish but have eternal life" (Jn. 3:16).

Gloria and Gordon,
Bless the Children
Ministry, Uganda,
2011

Gloria, Julie, Gordon, and Greg, Bless the Children
Ministry, Uganda, 2012

Top: Julie, Gloria, Greg, and Gordon, Bless
the Children Ministry, Uganda, 2013
Bottom: Gordon and Skyler, Tulsa
International Airport, 2012

Top: The Fuller Family, 2013
Bottom: The Fuller Family, 2014, Florida
vacation

Thank You

I'm so glad you read my story! If you enjoyed it, would you consider writing a review in *Amazon?* Thank you.

Contact

The Fuller family can be reached at: juliefuller918@gmail.com

Made in the USA
Columbia, SC
08 April 2018